Stories for the Offering

Stewardship meditations from everyday life

Jim Eichenberger

Edited by Theresa C. Hayes
Cover design by Robin Moro

Library of Congress Cataloging-in-Publication Data

Eichenberger, Jim
    Stories for the offering / Jim Eichenberger.
        p.   cm.
    ISBN 0-7847-0946-7
    1. Christian giving--Sermons. 2. Sermons, American. 3. Story sermons. 4. Offertories. I. Title.
    BV772.E43   1999
    264'.4--dc21   99-17831
                                          CIP

06   05   04   03   02   01   00   99   5   4   3   2   1

USING THIS BOOK

Jesus often began instructing his followers by telling a story. As we examine his words we will hear him say, "In a certain town . . ." or "There was a man who . . ." or even "Suppose one of you . . .".

The meditations in this book begin with simple stories—in most cases, the stories of experiences to which almost everyone will relate. After bringing hearers together on this *common* ground, speaker and listener can move together to *higher* ground, the authority of Scripture.

This book can be used in a number of ways. You might simply refer to the author and read the meditation as it is written. Another approach is for the speaker to change the first-person references (I, me, we) to third-person references (he, him, us) when using the devotion. But may we encourage another strategy?

In the margin of each meditation is a suggested way to "**Make it your own.**" We recommend that you personalize the meditation by sharing an experience *of your own* similar to that of the author. Since these stories relate incidents common to us all, this is usually a easy task.

The telling of simple stories has been used to effectively communicate complex truths for centuries. May you find this method helpful when you tell these **Stories for the Offering.**

CONTENTS

To those who have filled my life
with its richest stories and deepest joys—

my parents,
John and Kathleen,
and my daughters,
Rachel and Sarah.

Automatic

Laundry is one of the great mysteries of life for most men. We just don't understand it. We just assume it gets done somehow by someone.

One man I know of tells about his struggle with laundry during his college years. On occasion he would bring his dirty clothes home to his mother. In the interim, however, he had no choice but to do the wash himself.

Over a period of time, his mother remarked that his clothing appeared to become dingier and dingier. Concerned, she asked her son if he was using proper temperatures and if the load sizes and water levels were appropriate. He took her advice, but his laundry continued to become even more gray.

Finally, she brought him into the laundry room and asked him to demonstrate how he completed this task. She watched as he separated colors, set the proper wash cycles, and loaded the washer. As he began to walk away, she prompted, "Didn't you forget the detergent?"

Obviously taken aback he replied, "Detergent? I thought the machine dispensed that automatically."

We laugh at that attitude, but we often share it when it comes to the work of the church. "Give to missionaries? Give to the building fund? Give to support our paid staff? Don't those things just happen automatically?"

James, the brother of Jesus, fought that same "automatic" mind-set in the early church: "What good is it, my brothers, if a man claims to have faith but has no deeds? Can such faith save him? Suppose a brother or sister is without clothes and daily food. If one of you says to him, 'Go, I wish you well; keep warm and well fed,' but does nothing about his physical needs, what good is it? In the same way, faith by itself, if it is not accompanied by action, is dead" (James 2:14-17).

This time of the service is a reminder that we are called to respond in faith to the needs of this world. Do we believe God's work will be done automatically, or are willing to put action with our belief?

Make it Your Own

Think about it . . . We often assume something will work without considering how it really gets done. Did you ever have any strange idea about how a task was completed without considering your responsibility in it?

DATE USED _____

8

AVAILABLE

ACTS 3:2, 3, 6

The neighborhood children were at it again! Telling me about their new club, they radiated with excitement. They would recycle aluminum cans. They would sell craft items they made. They even planned a garage sale. All proceeds would go to charity. They called themselves, "Operation Help the World."

I smiled at their optimism. As I began to ask questions about their plans, I referred to their group as "Operation Save the World." This met with a stern reply from a serious nine-year-old. "No, it's 'Operation *Help* the World'."

Later, I understood the distinction. This hearty little band accomplished their goals. Five children, ages five through fourteen, raised money and purchased Russian language New Testaments for distribution after the breakup of the Soviet Union. Their work was the subject of a feature story in the Sunday edition of one of the state's most influential newspapers. They received a call from the White House and welcomed the Vice President when he came to town. Yet, they didn't save the world. They simply made themselves available to help in ways in which they were able.

A similar attitude was demonstrated by the early church. When Peter and John were asked for help by a lame man, they simply made what they had available to him. "Now a man crippled from birth was being carried to the temple gate called Beautiful, where he was put every day to beg from those going into the temple courts. When he saw Peter and John about to enter, he asked them for money. Then Peter said, 'Silver or gold I do not have, but what I have I give you. In the name of Jesus Christ of Nazareth, walk'" (Acts 3:2, 3, 6).

That same attitude is practiced in this congregation. We take what we have and make it available to those in need. We reach out our hands to help, allowing God to reach out his hand to save. May that be our attitude as we contribute to this offering.

Make it Your Own

Whom do you know who has made themselves available to help others? Perhaps some in your congregation have served quietly but effectively for years. Honor one of them by using his or her story to introduce these thoughts.

DATE USED _____

BREAD

I don't believe that I have ever eaten a slice of supermarket bread at Jim and Lori's house even though I have been a grateful recipient of their hospitality on countless occasions. It is simply that Lori is renowned for her homemade breads. Sourdough. Whole wheat. And that breakfast favorite, cinnamon raisin! It is not unusual to step inside their door and be met with that sweet, yeasty aroma.

Being a child of the 1960's, I have often used the word "bread" to mean something other than a pantry staple. Jim and Lori are known for their generosity with that kind of "bread" as well. Bountiful supporters of their church and many other worthy organizations, they choose to live simply and give wholeheartedly.

Solomon was a king known for his great wealth. But he was known even more for his wisdom. He knew that holding on to wealth was not profitable in the long run. In fact, the best way to be truly rich is to give. In the book of Ecclesiastes he advised, "Cast your bread upon the waters, for after many days you will find it again" (Ecclesiastes 11:1).

It seems foolish to throw bread into a river. Logic tells us to consume what we have, to keep our belongings for our own use. Yet God commands the ridiculous: to give, to give freely, to give in a way that a return on the investment appears unlikely. And yet God in his grace blesses such faith with even more blessings.

Each Sunday we pause to "cast bread upon the waters." Many here place a tenth and even more of their incomes into the care of this congregation. They expect nothing in return. They are purchasing nothing for themselves with this act. Yet I am sure that many could tell you that God has blessed this faithfulness many times over. Won't you join in this act of "sacrificial foolishness" during this moment of stewardship? Cast your bread upon the waters.

Make it Your Own

Whom do you know who lives a life marked with generosity? How has that person demonstrated faith in giving? Introduce this meditation with that story.

DATE USED _____

CHANGE

JOHN 9:8

Patty and I seemed to share a single brain at times. We laughed at the same jokes, enjoyed the same music, and watched the same movies. We comforted each other when our dating relationships soured, and we rejoiced together at our smallest victories. We were both extremely cynical, sneering at the conventional, the clichéd, and especially at the religious. We had no need of God or his church and never would. Or so we thought . . .

In our early twenties we began to go our own ways. After a few years we lost track of each other. In the meantime my life changed. I recognized the emptiness of my life and came to salvation in Jesus. Occasionally I prayed for Patty, but had no idea where she lived or what she was doing.

One Sunday morning when I was traveling, I attended the worship services in a small church in the Midwest. Running a little late that morning, I entered as services began and hurriedly found a seat. After a few opening songs, the worship leader asked that we all greet someone seated near us. I turned and stared directly into a familiar face. Patty and I spoke the same words simultaneously, "What are *you* doing here!" Later we met and discussed the tremendous changes that Jesus had made in our lives.

An encounter with Jesus always has and always will greatly alter the lives of individuals. John tells of the transformation of a blind man who had met the Lord. "His neighbors and those who had formerly seen him begging asked, 'Isn't this the same man who used to sit and beg?'" (John 9:8).

It is appropriate that we remind ourselves occasionally that the church is in the business of giving real people new lives. From this blind man of centuries ago to the person you are seated next to this morning, the work of Jesus continues. At this moment, as an act of worship, we all have the opportunity to participate in the ministry of changing lives as we bring our gifts to him.

Make it Your Own

The power and love of Christ reaches some very unlikely characters! Tell a conversion story to introduce this meditation.

DATE USED _____

Clean

I remember few of my part-time jobs as well as I recall my short-term employment with the *Lincoln Courier* during my college years. Needing a little extra income, I answered a want ad for a temporary maintenance position. My job, I discovered, was to give the plant its first thorough cleaning in decades.

The ink used in newspapers had found its way just about everywhere in the building. It formed the base of inch-thick sludge shrouding the machinery of the presses. It had been ground into the finish of every wooden desk in the news room. The old-fashioned venetian blinds were coated with a hardy layer of airborne ink vapor and dust. A similar alloy of filth had found a home around every door frame and window ledge. Day after day I would come home grimy and exhausted. But I had truly learned what it meant to clean.

The Pharisees of Jesus' day also knew how to clean. Jesus argued, however, that they did not understand how to *be* clean: "Then the Lord said to him, 'Now then, you Pharisees clean the outside of the cup and dish, but inside you are full of greed and wickedness. You foolish people! Did not the one who made the outside make the inside also? But give what is inside the dish to the poor, and every thing will be clean for you'" (Luke 11:39-41).

Sometimes we as Christians are like those Pharisees. We have a good idea about how to clean up our world, but we overlook our own sin. Notice that Jesus mentioned that giving to those in need was a mark of cleanliness. As we pause during this time of stewardship, let us consider our own cleanliness before God.

Make it Your Own

What was the messiest, filthiest cleaning job you ever tackled? Give all of the gritty details to introduce the content of this Scripture.

DATE USED _____

CONSIDERED

LUKE 21:1-4

At times I reflect upon the great inventions of man throughout history. From the wheel to the computer microchip, the list is impressive. But of all of these remarkable accomplishments, I am especially fond of one. Cruise control for my car.

Isn't it a wonderful device? I set the control and I cruise at a constant speed down the highway. I don't have to think about it. I am on "automatic pilot"!

Actually, I don't believe that any more. A few years ago, my cruise control malfunctioned. While driving through a quiet residential area, my car began to accelerate on its own! I recognized then that as convenient as it is to be on "automatic pilot," some activities, such as driving, require us to be ever alert to the consequences of our actions.

Another activity that requires vigilance is giving. Jesus pointed out the difference between automatic giving and duly-considered giving when he saw a poor widow at the temple. "As he looked up, Jesus saw the rich putting their gifts into the temple treasury. He also saw a poor widow put in two very small copper coins. 'I tell you the truth,' he said, 'this poor widow has put in more than all the others. All these people gave out of their wealth; but she out of her poverty put in all she had to live on'" (Luke 21:1-4).

Though I am not wealthy, it is easy for me to be like the rich people in this story. My giving is often on "cruise control." I set what I will give and do so automatically. And I just don't think about it any more.

The widow thought about her actions. She knew that she was giving what would other-wise supply her daily needs. She considered the faithfulness of God and his ability to care for the faithful. And then she gave.

During this time of stewardship, may we present only well-considered gifts. Let us take our giving off of "automatic pilot" and take time to meditate on what our faithful God would have us do for others.

Make it Your Own

What do you do habitually, auto-matically? Is there an area of your life that has been on "cruise control?"

DATE USED _____

CONSISTENCY

1 CORINTHIANS 16:1, 2

It was a shock when I picked up the paper from my front step that morning. Staring back at me . . . on the front page . . . above the fold . . . was MY FACE! The day before, a press photographer had covered the annual back-to-school routine at the school where I served as principal. I suspected that there would be a photo of our school somewhere in the paper, but there it was . . . there *I* was . . . on the front page. I was . . . a celebrity!

That day I basked in my newly-acquired fame. Students, parents, teachers, and friends greeted me with the honor accorded the near great. And what a day it was!

But the days following were quite different. My star had dimmed. The glory was gone, and in its place were all of the demands that accompanied my job. Although I had my time in the spotlight, that was now irrelevant. The message from my once-adoring public was unspoken but clear—"What have you done for me *lately*?!"

Life is like that. We are judged by the consistency of our day-to-day walk, not by our momentary sprints of accomplishment. The apostle Paul told the church in Corinth to recognize the necessity of that consistency in their generosity.

"Now about the collection for God's people: Do what I told the Galatian churches to do. On the first day of every week, each one of you should set aside a sum of money in keeping with his income, saving it up, so that when I come no collections will have to be made" (1 Corinthians 16:1, 2).

All aspects of our faith should be characterized by the constant glowing of the embers of our character, not by flashes of sporadic notoriety. During this time of the service each week we have the opportunity to demonstrate our generosity with simple consistency.

Make it Your Own

So when was your proverbial "15 minutes of fame?" Introduce this meditation with your story.

DATE USED _____

COOPERATION

ACTS 11:29

Have you ever noticed that nothing makes a project move more slowly than having your children "help" you perform it? My mother seemed to understand the secret of making those times productive, however.

I remember helping her make peanut butter cookies. Most of the job was hers. She mixed the dough, preheated the oven, and rolled the dough into balls of uniform size. I would place the dough on the cookie sheet and press the cookies flat with a fork. Because I had a specific duty that I was capable of performing, I truly was a help to my mother in completing her task. Although my part was small, I could honestly claim to have helped make those delicious cookies.

God's children certainly make a mess of things when we try to "help" him at times. Yet, when we are willing to perform small, specific duties according to our abilities, our Father can bring about great results.

Centuries ago, when the members of the church in Antioch heard of a coming famine, they wanted to help those affected by it. Luke records that, "The disciples, each according to his ability, decided to provide help for the brothers living in Judea" (Acts 11:29).

Every Lord's Day we have the opportunity to "help" our Father with his work throughout the world. Cooperatively, as we each give according to our abilities, we can share the satisfaction of sharing in a job well done.

Make it Your Own

How did you "help" your parents when you were a child? A story with either positive or negative results will work here.

DATE USED _____

22

Cost

Recently the florists in town sponsored a "Good Neighbor Day." They gave a dozen long-stem red roses to anyone who came in. The recipient of the flowers was to keep one and distribute the remaining eleven to friends, neighbors, and coworkers.

Being practical and frugal (some would say "cheap") both by nature and nurture, I saw a tremendous opportunity to be magnanimous. I have given flowers before and they were always received with enthusiastic gratitude. As I distributed a rose on that day, the response was less than I expected. Why? Simply because everyone knew that my gift had cost me nothing.

King David understood that same principle. When commanded to build an altar of sacrifice at a specific location, David went to the owner of the property to purchase that land. After he explained the reason for his purchase to Araunah, the landowner offered to give him the land at no charge. David responded, "No, I insist on paying you for it. I will not sacrifice to the Lord my God burnt offerings that cost me nothing" (2 Samuel 24:24).

Love that has no cost is not love. It is expedience. It is manipulation. Whenever we give in the hope that our investment will be less than our profit, we must rethink our actions.

Our model for giving is even greater than King David. The "Son of David," our Lord Jesus, gave at the greatest of costs.

When we give during this offering time we are doing more than superficially pretending to be "good neighbors." We are sharing ourselves by giving that which truly costs. In a small way we are modeling the love of Jesus.

Make it Your Own

Have you ever given a gift that cost you nothing? What was the response when the recipient found out?

DATE USED _____

Debt

I dreaded Wednesday and Thursday nights. Those were "collection nights" for me as a paperboy. I had to knock on about seventy doors a week, asking for payment for newspapers I had delivered on the preceding days. It was a time-consuming, often-frustrating task.

One customer continually fueled that frustration. Looking back, I am amazed at the variety of ways he avoided paying the debt he owed me. At times he simply refused to answer the door. On other occasions I was asked to return the next day at a specific time. Once in a while children were sent to the door to tell me that their father was busy. Now and then, he pulled a fifty-dollar bill from his wallet and feigned disappointment that I didn't have change. When the bill was particularly high, he chained his dog (which to this day I am sure was one part German shepherd and nine parts wolf) to the front porch, cutting off my approach. His arsenal of debt-avoidance techniques appeared limitless.

It is never pleasant to feel cheated of what is rightfully ours. For that reason, we as Christians should make every effort to have no outstanding debt. Addressing the church in Rome, the apostle Paul gave that counsel along with the single exception to the rule.

"Let no debt remain outstanding, except the continuing debt to love one another, for he who loves his fellowman has fulfilled the law" (Romans 13:8).

Our debt of love to others in this world is never fully paid. Each week during this time in the service we have the opportunity to "make a payment" on this outstanding bill. May this be a liability we never attempt to leave unpaid.

Make it Your Own

Everyone has had the experience of being cheated out of that which was rightfully theirs. Consider when that has happened to you. Tell about it to illustrate the point of this meditation.

DATE USED _____

DEFINITIONS

"I know three Jims," announced my three-year-old daughter with confidence.

"You do?" I responded.

"'Jim' is your name, Daddy."

"That's one."

"And there is your friend, Jim Cooper."

"That's two. Who is number three?"

A sparkle came to her eye as she announced, "Jim Nastics!"

Amused, I recalled that Brittina, a neighbor girl, had just been visiting and had demonstrated what she had learned in a gymnastics class. With a straight face, I played along. "So who is this Jim Nastics?"

"Oh, Daddy, you don't know him," came a nearly condescending reply. "He's Britt's jumping teacher."

We have all had trouble with definitions. Sometimes it is a word we have never heard before. Sometimes it is a word that is used often, but with a variety of meanings.

The word "righteous" is like the latter. People often define it according to their most treasured values. But listen to how God defines the word to his prophet Ezekiel:

"He does not oppress anyone, but returns what he took in pledge for a loan. He does not commit robbery but gives his food to the hungry and provides clothing for the naked. He does not lend at usury or take excessive interest. He withholds his hand from doing wrong and judges fairly between man and man. He follows my decrees and faithfully keeps my laws. That man is righteous; he will surely live, declares the Sovereign Lord" (Ezekiel 18:7-9).

At this time of the service it is appropriate to point out how much of that definition deals with stewardship of material goods. May we take care to define our terms as God does. May we seek to meet his definition of righteousness.

Make it Your Own

Everybody has a great story about a fractured definition. Tell yours instead of this one.

28

DATE USED —————

DISSENSION

I thumbed through the stack of baseball cards again. Where had it gone? My 1964 Lou Brock card had vanished!

I had been the envy of my neighborhood. For some reason, this card was rare among my fellow twelve-year-old collectors. I remembered the envy in the eyes of my friends as they had handled it the day before.

With the clarity of thought and singleness of purpose unique to an adolescent male, I began my crusade to return the hijacked treasure to my collection. With righteous anger, I banged on the doors of my friends houses, demanding the release of their cardboard captive.

My quest proved unsuccessful. Overshadowing that loss, however, was the damage that I had done to a close circle of friends. I not only alienated my buddies from me, but I also planted seeds of suspicion that would bear fruit of distrust for each other. And all for a one-cent piece of paper. . . .

When our focus is upon our material possessions, relationships grow strained. In trying to hold on to what is ours, we lose something much more valuable than our toys and trinkets.

Solomon observed this very truth: "A greedy man stirs up dissension, but he who trusts in the Lord will prosper" (Proverbs 28:25).

Every week at this time we have a corporate "priority check." Where are our ultimate values? I am convinced that Christians who trust God with their personal finances enjoy richer and more fulfilling relationships with their brothers and sisters in Christ. Is that the mark of our congregation?

Make it Your Own

Think back to a time when you became too focused upon a fairly insignificant material possession. What were the results? Tell the congregation about that experience.

30

DATE USED _____

Embarrassment

2 Corinthians 9:3, 4

It seemed like a good idea at the time. Rich and I were in chemistry class together. We hatched a practical joke aimed at Miss Smith, our teacher. It was daring. It was clever. It was fool-proof . . . or so we thought.

We were in chemistry class during first period every day. At the beginning of that hour the daily announcements were read over the public address system for all to hear. Discovering that placing an item on that never-questioned roster of memoranda was remarkably easy, we decided to prepare a bogus message for the daily list. I authored a totally spurious story about the presentation of the "Golden Test Tube Award" to Miss Smith from a fictional society of science educators. Rich affixed a very authentic-looking signature to the required submission form. All that was left to do was do sit back the next morning and watch our teacher's face when the announcement was read.

Her reaction was classic. Surprise, confusion, and annoyance ran across her face. Our gag was an enormous success . . . for the moment. But later that day we both received hall passes, inviting us to visit Miss Smith during her free period. The joke had worked too well. The school administration requested that she display her award in the trophy case. She had quickly agreed, delighting in the prospect of Rich and me scrambling to produce a sham statuette for display. With a test tube, glue, wood scraps and spray paint, we produced a crudely-fashioned trophy. That monument to our lack of preparation to face the consequences of our act was on display for the remainder of the year.

The church at Corinth was in a similar predicament. They had promised a large gift of benevolence, but as collection time came they were unprepared to follow through. Paul counseled, "But I am sending the brothers in order that our boasting about you in this matter should not prove hollow, but that you may be ready, as I said you would be. For if any Macedonians come with me and find you unprepared, we—not to say anything about you—would be ashamed of having been so confident" (2 Corinthians 9:3, 4).

Are we prepared to follow through on the commitments we make to God? Every week we have this opportunity to act upon our promises.

DATE USED _____

Make it Your Own

Consider a time in which your inability to meet the consequences of your actions caused embarrassment for you. Tell that story instead of this one.

ENTHUSIASM

2 CORINTHIANS 8:1, 3, 5

At a program for the day care center in which she worked, my daughter was introducing me to her students. Approaching a sweet, blonde four-year-old, she greeted her, "Hi, Stacy. This is *my* daddy."

Stacy flashed a shy smile my direction.

"Stacy," my daughter continued, "you know how you sing to me sometimes? Could you sing one of your songs to my daddy?"

I fully expected the preschooler to hide her face with embarrassment or perhaps haltingly whisper the words of a familiar children's chorus.

I was shocked beyond words when the tiny child looked me fully in the face and burst forth whole-heartedly, "Get me a ticket fo' an AIR-O-PLANE . . ." She continued for nearly two minutes, belting out two verses and the chorus of a song that was written when her parents were barely her age. By the time she reached the second refrain, I was singing with her, caught up in the excitement that she generated. "My BA-BEE, she wrote me a LETT-HER!"

33

What could we accomplish if we each had a fraction of the vitality of that child? The apostle Paul spoke of a group of believers who had a similar enthusiasm for the work of God:

"And now, brothers, we want you to know about the grace that God has given the Macedonian churches. For I testify that they gave as much as they were able, and even beyond their ability. And they did not do as we expected, but they gave themselves first to the Lord and then to us in keeping with God's will" (2 Corinthians 8:1, 3, 5).

What an endorsement! The churches in Macedonia were able to give "beyond their ability" because in their devotion "they gave themselves first to the Lord."

May this weekly time of stewardship be the mere aftermath of lives well lived before this morning. May people say of us that we give sacrificially because we have first whole-heartedly given ourselves to our God.

Make it Your Own

Children are always a great source of stories about enthusiasm. Do you recall a time in which a child was brimming with excitement for something he or she was doing? Tell it!

DATE USED _____

FLOOD

The phone rang at four o'clock in the morning. The voice of Dave, the school janitor, trembled in panicked tones. As he reported to work that morning, the results of that night's rainstorm greeted him in waves. The entire basement of the building was flooded.

I quickly dressed and met him at school. After making arrangements to hold affected classes in other parts of the building, I joined a small army of volunteers he had assembled to counter the damage. With mops and squeegees we contained the flood waters to one room. We constructed a makeshift dam of sandbags in the doorway and began to pump the water out of the room with ten wet/dry vacuum cleaners.

About three hours later we surveyed the damage. After emptying hundreds of gallons of water, it appeared that we had made no progress at all. When the heavens open and flood the earth with rain, the results are devastating!

The prophet Malachi also spoke about the bounties of Heaven coming to earth. Considering the results if Heaven's blessings were to be delivered to man, he commanded the people of Judah, "'Bring the whole tithe into the storehouse, that there may be food in my house. Test me in this,' says the Lord Almighty, 'and see if I will not throw open the floodgates of heaven and pour out so much blessing that you will not have room enough for it'" (Malachi 3:10).

Are we prepared for this type of flood? Are we willing to test God with our faithful giving? He is waiting to shower his people with blessings when they are faithful stewards of their belongings.

Make it Your Own

Nearly everyone has an experience with a flooded basement. This meditation will be particularly effective during a wet week in the spring!

DATE USED _____

FORGOTTEN

HEBREWS 13:16

It was a typical Sunday. Church service and Sunday school in the morning . . . a quick Sunday lunch . . . and off again, my wife to choir rehearsal, myself to a committee meeting. Because I had to run a quick errand before my meeting, we took separate cars.

After our obligations we met and walked to the church nursery together to pick up our daughter. When we arrived, we were shocked to find that our child was not there. We both turned to each other with, "I thought you. . . !"

Rushing home we found our daughter, still napping, unaware that she had been forgotten by the two people who loved her most! Embarrassment mixed with relief as we considered how our busy-ness had caused us to leave our infant unattended and alone for an hour.

It is easy in the rush of our busy lives to forget that which is most important. In the flurry of church activities in which we all participate, it is essential that we pause to take care of truly ministering to the people of God.

The writer of Hebrews warns us: "And do not forget to do good and to share with others, for with such sacrifices God is pleased" (Hebrews 13:16).

We can attend church services, go to meetings, and sing in the choir. We can teach Sunday school and visit the sick. All of these are important and should not be neglected. But in this rush of activity, do we forget to share with others?

Taking inventory of our personal belongings and determining to share a portion of them is an important part of worship. It is an appropriate action to take at this time.

Make it Your Own

We have all been so busy that we have forgotten something very important at one time or another. When has that happened to you?

DATE USED _____

Hoarding

In the simpler days of my childhood, a highlight of the year was going trick-or-treating. I remember returning home on a cool October evening and counting my tremendous wealth. I had amassed enough chocolate and processed sugar to last nearly forever—if I handled it right.

So I was very careful with what I had. I made a plan to eat only one piece a day, so that it would last. Then I stashed the bag of goodies out of the sight of my brother and sister so I wouldn't be distracted by their requests for my candy after theirs was gone.

Months later, my supply of sweets was nearly depleted. Funny how those last candy bars were really not all that satisfying. Their chocolate coatings were mottled with white patches. Once-crispy peanuts were remarkably stale. The caramel filling had attained the consistency of set concrete. Perhaps stockpiling candy was not that great of an idea after all.

The words of the prophet Amos spoke out against a similar mind-set in ancient Israel. "'They do not know how to do right,' declares the Lord, 'who hoard plunder and loot in their fortresses'" (Amos 3:10).

On a large or small scale, such actions are simply not right. Material wealth we have been granted is meant to be used compassionately, not stockpiled selfishly.

It is the practice of the members of this congregation to release a portion of our personal wealth each week. May we all find this to be a fulfilling way of dealing with that which our God grants us.

Make it Your Own

Do you recall a situation in which hoarding something backfired? Share that story in the place of this one.

DATE USED _____

IMITATION

2 CORINTHIANS 9:1, 2

It was a particularly dark day in my teaching career. By January of my first year as a ninth-grade teacher, exhaustion and frustration had drained me of enthusiasm and optimism.

Pouring my heart out to a colleague at lunch I whined, "I can't do this! They don't hear a word I say. They don't do anything I ask. I am just not getting through to my class!"

After listening to my tirade, she calmly replied, "Jim, have you noticed how your boys are wearing their hair?"

I felt my cheeks flush as bafflement gave way to anger. How dare she! My world was in crisis, and she wanted to discuss some insignificant breach of the dress code!

Responding to my hesitation, my fellow-teacher repeated her query. "Jim, why don't you take a look at how your boys are wearing their hair?"

In spite of myself, I complied with her request. As I surveyed the school cafeteria, I understood my colleague's counsel. In the course of my first four months of teaching, I had obviously made a much larger impression than I was aware. During that time all twelve of the fifteen-year-old boys in my class had begun to groom their hair in the same style in which I wore mine!

Whether we are aware of it or not, others learn from our example. They may imitate us in trivial matters, but they also may follow our lead in affairs of great consequence.

Paul told the church at Corinth that other believers were imitating their attitudes about giving. "There is no need for me to write to you about this service to the saints. For I know your eagerness to help, and I have been boasting about it to the Macedonians, telling them that since last year you in Achaia were ready to give; and your enthusiasm has stirred most of them to action" (2 Corinthians 9:1, 2).

When we give to our church, we have the opportunity to be a part of significant work in this community, our nation, and around the world. Let us encourage others to join us with our attitudes of enthusiasm.

DATE USED _____

Make it Your Own

Imitation is the sincerest form of flattery. Think of a time in which you were "flattered" in this way. Tell that story.

Imperishable

Nothing beats a home-cooked meal! A complete and nutritionally-balanced feast satisfies like nothing else. My family, like yours, I'm sure, responds enthusiastically when their favorites, hot from the oven, are placed before them.

But what happens when that delightful repast is not fully consumed? The uneaten food is carefully wrapped and placed in the refrigerator for another evening. Remarkably enough, those once mouth-watering victuals are then often viewed with contempt. They are given the singularly unappetizing label of "leftovers." My children took the insult one step further, calling them "gross food reruns."

Even the best of food may suffer from being stored and reheated. After a while food becomes less tasty, and eventually will spoil.

Jesus made reference to this fact when he taught his disciples about the value of the kingdom of God. "'Do not work for food that spoils, but for food that endures to eternal life, which the Son of Man will give you. On him God the Father has placed his seal of approval'" (John 6:27).

43

Of course, a good part of our paychecks go to purchase necessities for our families. But what a tragedy it would be if the only purpose of our labor was to pay for items that would, in the end, perish.

As members of this congregation we do not have to endure that futility. Each week we have the opportunity to demonstrate that we work for the eternal. With our tithes and offerings we are able to support ministries with everlasting results. We can buy "food that endures to eternal life."

Make it Your Own

This meditation can easily be used as is. But it could be enhanced if you had a story about food that had "gone bad" in your refrigerator. Try it.

DATE USED _____

INHERITANCE

Recently my daughter e-mailed me from college. It was "rush" week on campus, and the activities of the week disturbed her. She found the attitudes of those in fraternities and sororities toward those wishing to join them disquieting. She commented upon the humiliation heaped upon "rushees" by their potential "brothers" or "sisters" in the Greek societies.

She concluded her note by saying, "Daddy, I'm not even sure why I react so strongly to these attitudes. I know it's just meant to be fun, but it really bothers me. It must be the way I was raised."

I couldn't have been prouder. A fundamental sense of justice was a part of my daughter's character. She was repulsed by the idea of people using a position of power to humiliate the weak. Though she respected the work of these groups, she was able to question certain aspects of their traditions based upon her deeply-held values. And she recognized that those values were given to her by her parents.

In ancient Israel, all of the tribes except one had a physical inheritance to pass down to their children. Only the Levites had no land of their own to bequeath to future generations. But the Bible makes clear that they had a much different type of inheritance.

"The Lord said to Aaron, 'You will have no inheritance in their land, nor will you have any share among them; I am your share and your inheritance among the Israelites'" (Numbers 18:20).

The inheritance of the priestly tribe was greater than land or the wealth coming from it. Their heritage consisted of a unique relationship with Jehovah God.

As "a kingdom and priests" (Revelation 1:6) we as Christians have a similar inheritance to pass to future generations. We can bequeath a knowledge of our God and his ways. Through our gifts to this church we do more than finance programs. We, in a very real way, pass the values of our faith to succeeding generations.

Make it Your Own

Recall a time when your children demonstrated that they share your values. Share that recollection at this time.

DATE USED _____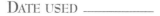

INTEGRITY

Early on a Saturday morning in August, they appeared at his door. The two men in dark suits identified themselves as FBI agents. They told my friend about the investigation they were pursuing.

They had just arrested a local investment banker for embezzlement. This investor had been entrusted with the retirement accounts of many people in our church. For years he had lied to his clients and falsified reports. But today the truth was known. Several clients, including my friend, had been swindled out of their life savings.

We live in a fallen world. The fact is, we must be cautious. Unscrupulous people exist who will attempt to cheat, lie, and steal to get what they want. If we are not careful stewards of our possessions, we could be easily relieved of them.

Realistically, we should be just as alert when those who claim to be Christians ask for our money. Will those responsible for the finances of the church behave with integrity?

The apostles addressed that very issue in the early days of the church. When they were confronted with the charges of inequity in the distribution of church funds, there were no attempts of cover-up or denial. Instead they devised a system of appointing accountable and honest men to be in charge of church finances. "'Brothers, choose seven men from among you who are known to be full of the Spirit and wisdom. We will turn this responsibility over to them'" (Acts 6:3).

This model is followed in this congregation today. Leaders known to be full of the Holy Spirit and wisdom are chosen to distribute the funds of this body of believers. It is important to know that the gifts we give at this point of the service are used with integrity.

Make it Your Own

Have you ever been cheated? Most everyone will be able to relate to or sympathize with that story. Use it to introduce this meditation.

DATE USED _____

LEAST

When I was attending college, my wife and I lived in a public housing complex. The apartments around us were filled with small children. Having a soft spot in my heart for children, I would pause to speak to my young neighbors on my way to and from work and school. I would patiently listen to stories about their pets. I would comment upon the stylishness of their new shoes or shirt. Occasionally a little one would run to me and present me with a fresh-picked dandelion from the small tract of green that surrounded the apartments. I would dutifully slide the stem of the yellow flower into a buttonhole and wear it proudly.

My wife was amused at the bond that developed between me and my young "playmates." She was less than amused, however, when a delegation of the neighborhood gang came to the door and asked her, "Can your *son* come out to play?"

The teachings of Jesus are filled with commands to attend to the needs of individuals, especially the needs of ones easily overlooked by others. Near the end of his ministry he spoke of those who would receive eternal rewards: "Then the King will say to those on his right, 'Come, you who are blessed by my Father; take your inheritance, the kingdom prepared for you since the creation of the world. For I was hungry and you gave me something to eat, I was thirsty and you gave me something to drink, I was a stranger and you invited me in, I needed clothes and you clothed me, I was sick and you looked after me, I was in prison and you came to visit me.'

'I tell you the truth, whatever you did for one of the least of these brothers of mine, you did for me'" (Matthew 25:34-36, 40).

The church of Jesus Christ is commanded to care for "the least of these." It is our job to bring strength to the weak, comfort to the afflicted, and companionship to the abandoned.

Each week, as a body of believers, we commit a portion of our resources to fulfill that command. A portion of this offering will go to meet needs of those a self-absorbed society easily ignores. Join with us as we care for "the least of these."

Make it Your Own

Recall a time in which you ministered to young children, the elderly, the ill, or others who could be considered "the least of these." Tell about your experience.

DATE USED _____

LOAN

Interest rates were high. Our savings were low to non-existent. Yet the house we had our eye on was just the right size and in such a great location. We could picture our daughters in their own bedrooms. The living room and dining rooms were perfect for entertaining. I could walk to work and the kids could walk to school were we to buy this house. But how could we afford it?

A friend was aware of our plight. He gathered a group of friends together and described our situation to them. From that meeting he came to us with a welcome offer. This committee of friends was able to put together enough cash to supply us with a down payment for our house. We would repay the loans at no interest over a period of a few years. We moved into our first house within months of that offer of a loan.

Most of us have benefited from a loan from a friend. Maybe it was the loan of money. Maybe it was the loan of a vehicle, clothing, or other needed objects. Regardless, it was an act of generosity that was based upon love and trust.

In the book of Proverbs, Solomon speaks

of making a loan to the best Friend of all. He spoke of how we can loan money to God. "He who is kind to the poor lends to the Lord, and he will reward him for what he has done" (Proverbs 19:17).

When we give charitably, we are lending our wealth to the Father of all blessings. The capital is secure in the hands of the divine. He will pay us back.

During this point of the service we pause to consider the stewardship of that which is not truly ours in the first place. Join with us now as we give to those in need. Join with us now as we make a loan to our God. Can we think of a more trustworthy borrower? Never has an investment been more secure.

Make it Your Own

Nearly everyone has benefited from a loan from a friend. When has someone made such a loan to you? What was it? How did you benefit?

DATE USED _____

Measurement

"Why not build it rather than buy it?"
That's what I was thinking when I decided
to put a small bulletin board in my child's
room. I purchased a section of cork board,
some nice oak strips, and varnish. I carefully
measured the cork and cut the lumber at
precise forty-five degree angles with the
help of my miter box, so that the corners of
the frame would meet at perfect right
angles.

My technique was flawless . . . almost. I
had made one tiny mistake. I had measured
the outside of my frame rather than the
smaller inside dimensions. As a result, I had
created a frame too small for the bulletin
board. Both my efforts and my materials
were wasted.

It occurred to me that this lesson had
application far beyond woodworking. I
thought of times when I assessed the merit
of something in my life inaccurately. As a
result, I always squandered something of
value.

Jesus made that observation to a man
who measured the worth of his family
wrongly:

"Someone in the crowd said to him, 'Teacher, tell my brother to divide the inheritance with me.'

Jesus replied, 'Man, who appointed me a judge or an arbiter between you?' Then he said to them, 'Watch out! Be on your guard against all kinds of greed; a man's life does not consist in the abundance of his possessions'" (Luke 12:13-15).

As in Jesus' day, people still use material goods as a measuring stick. When we do that, however, we often "come up short" in life. During this time of the service, we can reevaluate our means of measurement. We do that when we surrender a portion of our belongings for something of much greater value, the work of our God on this earth.

Make it Your Own

Have you ever made a similar measuring mistake? It could have been in carpentry, construction, gardening, cooking, or almost any other discipline. Tell about the results of that error when you present this meditation.

DATE USED _____

NAMES

My parents had just returned from a shopping trip with my two daughters, then aged 3 and 7. They went out to pick up some necessities, so they returned home with two dolls that their grandchildren just "had" to have.

The girls proudly displayed their fabric and yarn progeny and told me all about them. When I asked my younger child her baby's name, it was obvious that she did not have a ready answer. Pausing thoughtfully, she glanced down at the tag sewn into the body of the toy. Clearly she thought that the tag would hold the name of her doll. She asked her older sister to read the label aloud, thereby revealing the identity of her charge.

She couldn't have been more pleased with the words that were read. In fact, to this very day we all fondly refer to that rag doll by the elegant and exotic name my daughter *thought* her sister had read. This polyester-filled princess will always be known as "Maiden," her full name being, of course, *"Maiden Haun Cong."*

The people of Israel misused names in a less humorous manner. They allowed practices ordained by their God to become something quite different than what the original "Labeler" intended. The prophet Isaiah took them to task over what they would call a "fast day:"

"'Yet on the day of your fasting, you do as you please and exploit all your workers. Your fasting ends in quarreling and strife, and in striking each other with wicked fists. Is that what you call a fast, a day acceptable to the Lord?

'Is not this the kind of fasting I have chosen: to loose the chains of injustice and untie the cords of the yoke, to set the oppressed free and break every yoke? Is it not to share your food with the hungry and to provide the poor wanderer with shelter?'" (Isaiah 58:3, 4, 6, 7).

We label this part of the service "offering." Is this name accurate? Let us examine our personal stewardship at this time, making sure that what we do truly lives up to the label we give it.

Make it Your Own

A story about a misunderstood name or a misread label of your own could be easily inserted here.

56

DATE USED _____

NEGLECT

Quite frankly, I don't like going to the dentist. The very mention of the word conjures visions of screaming drills, mouthfuls of gauze, and needle-sharp picks seeking the most sensitive areas of my gums. Yes, doctor, I'll tell you in advance. It *does* hurt!

For that reason I avoided making my six-month appointment . . . for about ten years! At the end of that time, prodded by alternating dull aches and white-hot flashes of pain in my molars, I visited the dreaded office.

Dr. Sherman, a man of few words and dry wit looked me coolly in the eye after that long overdue session. "So," he droned dispassionately, "How long would you like to keep your real teeth?"

I did keep my teeth, but learned an important lesson. Sometimes we neglect small duties and bring about painful results. Though I justified my neglect by saying that I was too busy with the big tasks of life to have time for check-ups and dental floss, the fact was, I needed to make time for both.

Jesus chided the leaders of his day for

neglecting the true responsibilities of God's people. "'Woe to you, teachers of the law and Pharisees, you hypocrites! You give a tenth of your spices—mint, dill and cummin. But you have neglected the more important matters of the law—justice, mercy and faithfulness. You should have practiced the latter, without neglecting the former'" (Matthew 23:23).

It is not difficult to superficially practice the rituals and routines of faith while neglecting their purpose. The teachers and Pharisees were great bookkeepers, but did not take the time to truly give.

During this time of offering we do more than "balance the books" with God by paying him what we "owe" him. We allow ourselves and the ministries supported by this congregation to be forces for "the more important matters of the law—justice, mercy and faithfulness."

Make it Your Own

What have you neglected? Was it a dental visit? A car repair? A kind word or apology? Describe your neglect and the results instead of using this story.

DATE USED _____

NEVER-ENDING

DEUTERONOMY 15:11

My hands recoiled from the hot, soapy water. Slowly, cautiously, I submerged them again. The flush on my face had less to do with the heat on my hands than the frustration in my heart. Was there anything as futile as performing family dish washing duty?

Night after night that week I had tackled a stack of dirty dishes. And what was the reward for my labor twenty-four hours later? Another stack, just as tall, just as dirty. "*Hey!*" I cried. "We could *keep* a clean dish in this house, if people weren't *eating* every day!"

This probably wasn't the stupidest thing I have ever said in my life, but is certainly comes close. Clean dishes were only a means to an end. That end was making sure that the family was fed. Not eating so that dishes would stay clean would have been a ludicrous reversal of priorities.

You know, I confess I have felt similar frustration at offering time. Every week I write a check and put it in the plate. A week later, I do the same thing. Will it ever end? I am almost tempted to cry out, "Hey! We wouldn't need to always take an offering in this church if we didn't keep giving money away to people who needed it!"

Listen to what Moses said to the Israelites about giving. "There will always be poor people in the land. Therefore I command you to be openhanded toward your brothers and toward the poor and needy in your land" (Deuteronomy 15:11).

The purpose of giving is no more for the purpose of having a full church treasury any more than the purpose of doing dishes is for the purpose of having pristine, but unused, eating utensils. We have been called by God to be his instruments in meeting a constant, pressing need of society. Let us react to this privilege with joy rather than frustration.

Make it Your Own

Can you think of another never-ending task you have performed? How did you feel about it? What was its ultimate purpose? Tell that story instead of this one.

DATE USED _____

OBLIGATION

No two children are exactly alike. Nevertheless, I had not seen children that differed more than James and Daniel. Though they were in the same fourth grade class, they shared little else in common.

The intellectual ability of James was obvious, even at a young age. He was remarkably different from his classmates. He had mastered the game of chess before most of his peers had even heard of it. His grasp of current events compelled him to attempt to discuss domestic and foreign policy issues with nine-year olds who simply stared at him with a mixture of apathy and irritation.

Daniel, on the other hand, had only a minimum of academic ability. His reading skills were below grade-level, his attention span was short, and his answers to the simplest questions were "inventive," to put it kindly.

So which of these two students was the school to serve? James required little effort to teach, since he absorbed and processed information with computer-like efficiency. Daniel was difficult to instruct, yet his need obviously called for our attention. To which would we attend? The answer, of course, is that we were called to care for both, and everyone in between.

To whom are we called to bring the gospel of Christ? Do we seek to save the "good" people who are looking for an enduring standard on which to base their morality? They certainly seem to be the least threatening individuals whom to approach. But what about those who have nearly destroyed their lives with reckless living? Their need for God's Word is painfully apparent. To whom should we attend? The answer, of course, is that we are called to share with both, and everyone in between.

Make it Your Own

Do you remember two very different children in your class when you attended school? How about students that you have taught in Sunday school? Tell about them to introduce this meditation.

The apostle Paul told the church at Rome, "I am obligated both to Greeks and non-Greeks, both to the wise and the foolish" (Romans 1:14).

To whom is this congregation obligated? We must agree with Paul. A world filled with both "the wise and the foolish" has need of the good news of a savior. Tithes and offerings given to our church serve both those earnestly seeking God and those in most desperate need of him.

DATE USED _____

PRETENSE

As the first grandchild on both sides of the family, my daughter attained instant celebrity status. She received attention from relative after relative. She had the wardrobe of a princess due to an out-of-control "I-saw-that-and-it-was-soooooooo-cute-I-just-had-to-buy-it" binge of family and friends. And, of course, there were the toys. . . .

If it squeaked, spun, wound, or whined, it was hers. A stuffed animal menagerie inhabited her crib. And her dolls could have populated the maternity ward of a fair-sized hospital!

One day I noticed her maternally cradling a bundle wrapped in a blanket. When I asked her which baby she was holding, she replied, "Kinkle." Not sure which of her brood went by that strange name, I peeked inside the blanket. Instead of seeing one of her many dolls, I saw a meat-tenderizing mallet that she had found on the kitchen counter!

Children delight in pretending. In their imaginations their worlds are transformed and they are transported to places far away and exotic.

63

A habit of pretense continues into adulthood, with results that are far less harmless. Solomon talked about the ways people pretend when it comes to what they own. "One man pretends to be rich, yet has nothing; another pretends to be poor, yet has great wealth" (Proverbs 13:7).

How true! We often pretend to have more than we truly own to impress others. Yet, when we are asked to share that which we *do* have, isn't it easy to feign poverty?

Let's outgrow our pretentions. At this time of the service, may we be realistic about our material blessings, and generous in how we share them.

Make it Your Own

Were you imaginative as a child? Tell one of your stories instead of this one.

DATE USED _____

PROPORTION

My dad used to love drawing at the family dinner table. After an evening meal, he would take his carpenter's pencil and sketch directly on the Formica tabletop. Although his masterpieces were short-lived (they would vanish when mom cleared the dishes and wiped off the table), they impressed me enough to try my hand at sketching as well.

Something was terribly wrong with my first doodles, however. The sketches of people I created lacked the realism of my father's work. Try as I might, all I could draw was a cast of awkward, clumsy-looking characters.

Perplexed, I showed my work to my dad. He immediately identified my problem as one of proportion. He taught me a few "tricks of the trade." I learned that a person's ear extends from the top of his eyebrow to the bottom of his nose. I learned that the height of the remainder of a person's body is about five times that of the height of his head. With these and a few other tips, my drawing greatly improved. In proper proportion, the people I sketched attained a lifelike quality they once lacked.

A sense of proportion is obvious when we look at our appearance. Not everyone has the same size mouth, but we have mouths that are proportionate to the size of our faces. We do not have the same size heads, but we have heads that are in proportion to the height of the rest of our bodies.

Proportion is also an important concept when it comes to generosity. Not everybody can give the same size gifts, but we can give gifts of value proportionate to our earnings. Moses explained this to the nation of Israel in this way: "Each of you must bring a gift [to God] in proportion to the way the Lord your God has blessed you" (Deuteronomy 16:17).

We follow that command to this day. When our giving is proportionate to our blessings, the body of Christ is not a crudely drawn cartoon, but a masterpiece of realism and true beauty.

Make it Your Own

Who taught you to draw? Did you learn similar lessons of proportion? Tell that story. You may even wish to illustrate it for effect!

DATE USED _____

REFRESHMENT

PROVERBS 11:25

No two people I have ever known love kids more than Ron and Mary Ann. They have dedicated their lives to serving elementary school age children. For more than thirty years this dedicated couple comprised the entire staff of a small church-operated elementary school in a small midwest town. Each year Ron would teach about twenty fourth through eighth graders. Mary Ann would instruct nearly an equal number of younger students. Ron served as principal and coach in addition to teaching duties. Mary Ann handled clerical and nursing duties for the school.

It often saddened me to think that these two beautiful servants were never blessed with children of their own.

One evening I joined others at their modest home. During an informal meal, we ran short of drinks. Seated closest to the kitchen, I volunteered to get the other pitcher of tea from the refrigerator.

Walking into the kitchen, I immediately realized that my sadness for Ron and Mary Ann's childless household was unjustified. The refrigerator was completely covered with "family" memorabilia. Homemade crafts, school pictures, notes, and scribbled pictures torn from coloring books nearly obscured that major appliance. No, the couple had not one child of their own, but they literally had hundreds! The children whose lives they touched as teachers stayed close to them long after they left the school.

The sacrificial lifestyle led by these two had been amply rewarded with the treasure they most desired. The words of King Solomon came to mind: "A generous man will prosper; he who refreshes others will himself be refreshed" (Proverbs 11:25).

As we pause to collect an offering this morning, let us recall this relevant proverb. We serve a God who greatly rewards a generous spirit.

Make it Your Own

Whom do you know that has lived a generous lifestyle? How were they refreshed by others?

DATE USED _____

SECRETS

MATTHEW 6:3, 4

Although I was at church, my mind was far away. The financial impact of having a newborn in the house had hit with explosive force. While my feet walked toward the sanctuary, my head reeled with the aftershocks of bill upon bill that I had opened that week.

A tap on my shoulder broke into my brooding. The minister handed me an envelope and said, "This was left in the church office for you." I took the card, obviously a note of congratulations on the birth of my daughter, and slid it into the pocket of my jacket.

After worship I returned home. Taking off my jacket, I removed the card I had placed there. The expected "Congratulations!" was embossed in pink on the outside of the greeting, but inside I found a totally unexpected shade of green. In amazement I counted the small stack of crisp bills contained in the unsigned missive. The bill collector's demands were met, almost to the penny!

In the years that followed, I have seen my needs and the needs of others met in similar fashion. Silently and namelessly, saints of God have come to the aid of others.

Such is the power of obedience to our Lord's command: "But when you give to the needy, do not let your left hand know what your right hand is doing, so that your giving may be in secret" (Matthew 6:3, 4).

When these gifts that are collected now are distributed, it will be without fanfare and without recognition of the contributor. The work of our God will quietly continue, with only him receiving the glory.

Make it Your Own

Do you recall receiving an anonymous gift? Tell about it in the context of this meditation.

DATE USED _____

SECURITY

Walking to my door in the summer twilight, I began to feel uneasy. Something was wrong. Then I noticed the door of the garage slightly opened, the hasp and lock torn out of the wood. Someone had broken in.

Rushing inside, I told my wife what I had seen. We went to the garage together, confirming that two new bicycles had been taken.

A knot formed in my stomach and my cheeks began to burn with indignation and frustration. "What does it take to protect our belongings?" I shouted. We lived in a nice neighborhood. The garage was secured with a tamper-resistant padlock. Yet, armed with only a crowbar, a brazen burglar had entered our world during the daylight hours, even though someone was in the house less than twenty feet away! What *can* we do to hold on to what we own?

The answer was obvious. "Not a thing." No security precautions can guarantee that our property will remain in our possession. Locks can be broken. Alarms can be bypassed. Watchdogs can be outwitted.

Anything we own can be taken from us at *any time*.

The words of Jesus were never more clear. "Do not store up for yourselves treasures on earth, where moth and rust destroy, and where thieves break in and steal. But store up for yourselves treasures in heaven, where moth and rust do not destroy, and where thieves do not break in and steal. For where your treasure is, there your heart will be also" (Matthew 6:19-21).

As we release a portion of our earnings during this offering time, may we understand this fact. We are not losing this gift. We are putting it in the only place where it is truly secure.

Make it Your Own

Recall a time when you lost a prized possession. Substitute that story for this one.

DATE USED _____

SWEAT

1 THESSALONIANS 2:9

For years my exercise regimen consisted of a morning run. I would rise before the rest of my family and "hit the bricks" for a few miles. My morning constitutional would energize me and get me prepared for the day ahead.

One morning, my daughter, then about four years old, was up when I returned. I approached her to give a good morning hug. She took one look at me and pulled back. "Daddy," she scolded, "you are one sweaty man!"

A healthy sweat is a mark of serious work having been accomplished. We work up a sweat with vigorous exercise or with arduous physical labor. Our sweat indicates our earnestness and our zeal.

The apostle Paul expended a great deal of sweat on behalf of the churches to whom he ministered. He toiled tirelessly for new believers in newly-established congregations. When writing to Christians in Thessalonica, he reminded them of this fact. "Surely you remember, brothers, our toil and hardship; we worked night and day in order not to be a burden to anyone while we preached the gospel of God to you" (1 Thessalonians 2:9).

Paul knew that God's gift of salvation was free. He wanted to convince others of this fact. Therefore, he accepted no payment from those whom he was attempting to win to Christ. This meant the burden of sacrifice fell to him.

This church shares a similar philosophy. We are involved in spreading the gospel in many ways throughout the world. We wish to do so at no cost to those we are winning. To do that takes sacrifice. It takes "sweat." During this time of stewardship we demonstrate our earnestness and zeal for those who do not know Jesus. Join with us in this act of dedication and compassion at this time.

Make it Your Own

What makes you work up a good sweat? Exercise? A grueling physical task? Think of such a time and tell that story.

DATE USED _____

74

TALK

Lately my mailbox has been filled with great news! I may already be a winner of millions of dollars. Within months a celebrity spokesperson could be at my door with a gigantic check. Video cameras will record my reaction to my new wealth.

Let me tell you a little bit of what I will say on that grand occasion. Sure, I'm going to treat myself to some of the things I've always wanted. But I won't be selfish. I've got special gifts in mind for family and friends. And I'm going to take care of those who really need help.

On that day my Christian witness will be obvious to all. Those Bible translators in third world countries will get my support. And I'm going to be generous with that hospital in India. Yes, I really want to do something for that children's home we always talk about. Of course, I certainly won't forget the needs of this local congregation.

I've got great plans. My generosity will know no bounds. Just wait. When my ship comes in, everyone I know will be well-provided for.

Years ago Solomon spoke of my attitude. "Like clouds and wind without rain is a man who boasts of gifts he does not give" (Proverbs 25:14).

Ouch! Solomon recognized that promises about gifts that one never gives is useless noise. Wind that brings no rain. . . .

Each week at this time we have the opportunity to do more than just talk. Instead of speaking about what we would like to do "only if," we can bring renewal and refreshment to others through our generosity today.

Make it Your Own

Bring a copy of a sweepstakes mailing you have received recently. Read it to introduce these thoughts.

DATE USED _____

THIRST

Having been born and raised in the midwest, I had never heard of Santa Ana winds. These devastating gusts are well known by residents of Los Angeles and vicinity, however.

On occasion these winds buffet the coast of southern California. Dry desert air rushes from high inland plateaus and is heated by compression. It is said that these winds can reduce snow or ice to water vapor without first melting it. During Santa Anas, dry brush spontaneously bursts into flame. The dry conditions are reported to have similar effects on human emotions.

Several years ago I visited relatives in that part of the country. As we drove through the area, it seemed that my hosts were stopping nearly every block to purchase something to drink. Before long I felt like I could not consume another drop. Yet they continued to down one soft drink after another.

A day later I experienced sensations unlike any I had in the past. Partially dehydrated, I was weak, unfocused, and irritable. I learned that thirst is more than a dryness in the throat. A lack of drink can drain body, mind, and spirit.

Jesus understood thirst. He described relieving the thirst of another believer as a fundamental act of kindness. "I tell you the truth, anyone who gives you a cup of water in my name because you belong to Christ will certainly not lose his reward" (Mark 9:41).

The offering we take each week meets a variety of needs. One of those is to offer "a cup of water" to Christian servants who labor for our Lord in a variety of ways. This congregation helps support those who minister in this location as well as others who serve around the world. Our gifts help to revitalize these courageous men and women who exhaust themselves daily as they work for Jesus. I encourage you to join in this act of kindness at this time.

Make it Your Own

Have you ever been really thirsty? Use your story to introduce these thoughts.

78

<small>DATE USED</small> _____

TRADITION

My family was big on tradition. Our established observances were not necessarily grand, important events. Some were small, seemingly mundane. But I recall them fondly to this day.

One tradition was "popcorn night." Wednesday night. Every Wednesday night. Without fail, Mom would pop a washbasin full of fluffy white corn and deliver it to Dad. We would fill our bowls from the basin and pour a glass of soda for ourselves. (Popcorn night was the only evening when were allowed to drink pop.) Then all of us would settle down in front of the television and watch the Dick van Dyke Show.

Though this tradition may seem inconsequential, the memories are still fresh. A warm feeling of a family gathered together . . . a security in knowing that the event would take place without exception. . . . To this day I cannot hear the theme music of the classic sitcom that we viewed together without experiencing a buttery, salty sensation on my lips.

Traditions bring us together. They unite us in a common task. They assure us with their

79

regularity. They build memories that are rich and indelible.

The church is rich with tradition. Paul wrote to the church in Thessalonica, "Therefore, brethren, stand fast, and hold the traditions which ye have been taught, whether by word, or our epistle" (2 Thessalonians 2:15, *KJV*).

A tradition that this congregation observes is to take a weekly offering. While this act may be simple, it is profoundly significant. The observance transcends the simple feat. We are united in purpose as we reach out together. We establish an identity as a caring loving people that will last long after this moment passes. Join us in partaking in this very significant tradition of our church family.

Make it Your Own

What family tradition from your childhood do you recall? Tell that story in the place of this one.

DATE USED _____

UNCERTAINTY

JAMES 4:13-15

Jason was a remarkable ten-year-old. Diagnosed with leukemia months before, he endured the hair loss, the outrageous appetite, and other side effects of chemotherapy with strength, grace, and apparent victory. His doctors had announced in the spring that his cancer had gone into remission.

Yet I stood before my school board that September evening and announced that the disease had now returned. I further reported that I had arranged with Jason's parents to give him a day off of school the following day. The two of us would travel to Chicago to watch our beloved Cubs. The board thanked me for my concern. Lew, one of the younger, more enthusiastic members, spoke to me privately, offering to help me with the expenses of the trip. Declining, I thanked him for his interest and generosity.

Jason beat the odds. Months later the cancer again retreated and has yet to return. Ironically, the eve of our baseball pilgrimage was the last time I spoke to my friend, Lew. He died of a heart attack that evening.

In the grief of the days that followed, I reflected upon the uncertainties of mortality.

One life, though attacked by disease, survived. Another, though in apparent health, was lost. James, the brother of Jesus, spoke of the unpredictable, temporary nature of our lives. "Now listen, you who say, 'Today or tomorrow we will go to this or that city, spend a year there, carry on business and make money.' Why, you do not even know what will happen tomorrow. What is your life? You are a mist that appears for a little while and then vanishes. Instead, you ought to say, 'If it is the Lord's will, we will live and do this or that'" (James 4:13-15).

We often look to our business and our finances for stability. James points out the foolishness of such a view. Certainty is found only in conforming to the will of our ever-faithful God.

Each week at this point of the service we back up that affirmation with action. Our earnings, as important as they are, are not sufficient. We trust not in them, but in the grace of our God. Let us make that same bold statement as we give our tithes and offerings now.

Make it Your Own

Life is uncertain. What event has made you aware of your own mortality? If you are able to share that story, it could be a powerful way to begin this meditation.

DATE USED _____

URGENCY

PSALM 132:1-5

As a young man, I had one true love of my life. She was beautiful. I gave my full attention to her every need. I spent every minute I could with her. I would caress her tenderly and pamper her endlessly. She was, of course, my first car, a 1964 Dodge convertible.

Owning a convertible was great. Even during the winter months in central Illinois, I dreamt of driving down the road, wind blowing through my hair, radio turned up to an eardrum-rupturing volume. I would watch the weather reports with a sense of urgency. Whenever a sunny day with temperatures over 40 degrees was forecast, I would spring into action. The top would come down and off I would drive, the car heater huffing ineffectually against the Arctic tempest.

Those days are gone. While I do not miss freezing in a drafty convertible, I do miss that passion I had for that first car. Does anything hold my attention and devotion like that today?

King David would have had a ready answer to that question. His answer would be, "Doing the work of the Lord."

"O Lord, remember David and all the hardships he endured. He swore an oath to the Lord and made a vow to the Mighty One of Jacob: 'I will not enter my house or go to my bed—I will allow no sleep to my eyes, no slumber to my eyelids, till I find a place for the Lord, a dwelling for the Mighty One of Jacob'" (Psalm 132:1-5).

Is our sense of urgency similar to that of David's? Do we seek with enthusiasm to serve our God as David did? How we prioritize our time and our income is a great indicator of our passion for him.

Make it Your Own

What monopolized your time when you were younger? A car? Clothes? Sports? Express the passion you felt instead of using this story.

DATE USED _____

VISION

Within two days time, I nearly fell down the steps ten times, spilled my drink at dinner twice, bumped into five complete strangers while walking in a local shopping center, and developed a world-class headache to accompany an excruciating stiffness in my neck.

Was I ill? Had I developed some sort of debilitating handicap? Was I experiencing a severe reaction to medication? No. I was simply adjusting to my new bifocals.

The first forty-eight hours of wearing this badge of middle-age had obvious effects. But as time passed, my vision adjusted. I began to see more clearly than I had in a long time.

When he was imprisoned in Rome, the apostle Paul had a spiritual "bifocal experience." His vision began to adjust, and he started seeing life better than ever before.

"I know what it is to be in need, and I know what it is to have plenty. I have learned the secret of being content in any and every situation, whether well fed or hungry, whether living in plenty or in want.

I can do everything through him who gives me strength" (Philippians 4:12, 13).

How is our vision? Have we learned the secret of contentment in and dependence upon our Lord Jesus, or are we still tripping over the harsh realities of life? Are our eyes still focused upon the temporary and the material, or has our spiritual sight been adjusted, allowing us to see a more complete picture of God's purpose and grace? Our response to this time in this service can serve as a very effective "eye test" for us.

Make it Your Own

Do you have an eyeglasses story? How about an experience in which your vision was temporarily distorted by eyedrops or by injury? Talk about that time to introduce these thoughts.

DATE USED _____

WEAK

PSALM 41:1

As the principal of a church-related school, I always enjoyed sharing the excitement of parents of newly-enrolled students. One year, weeks before school was to begin, such a mother phoned to discuss school supplies. Though it was barely July, she was giving me a complete list of purchases she had made for the upcoming September adventure. Suddenly during the monologue I heard her speak the words, "Oh, yes, and my kids have HIV."

Immediately the circuit boards of my brain, once buzzing drowsily with polite responses to the mundane, were jammed with emergency signals. *Are we prepared for this? Will we be able to adequately protect these children and those around them? How and to whom do I communicate the news of this serious health problem?*

As I regained my composure, I discovered that I had misunderstood. My new students were not infected with a deadly virus. The excited mother simply misspoke. I soon realized she was talking about the version of the Bible her children had for school. She meant to say "N-I-V," not "H-I-V"!

I often think of the feelings of panic I felt, if only for moments, on that day. Though I would like to believe that I would always deal compassionately with those tragically afflicted, how would I act when truly having to face the prospect of enrolling students with AIDS into our church school? After hanging up to phone, I began the first draft of a policy to follow on such an occasion. I began to make a plan of compassionate action long before such a crisis hit.

King David has encouragement for those who care about the weak and afflicted. "Blessed is he who has regard for the weak; the Lord delivers him in times of trouble." (Psalm 41:1).

Make it Your Own

How do you work for the benefit of the weak and needy? What led you to act the way you do? Was a particular event instrumental in spurring you into action? Introduce this devotion with that story.

As good-hearted as we would like to believe we are, our human nature tends toward selfishness and self-preservation. It is helpful to think about what we need to do with regard to the weak long before we are asked to help in a specific situation. This time of stewardship is such an opportunity. We can be a part of this congregation's well-considered plan to reach out to those who are in need.

DATE USED _____

NEW

(SUITABLE FOR NEW YEAR'S)
LAMENTATIONS 3:22, 23

A few months ago I drove my daughter to the airport to catch an early flight. Arriving early, we checked her bags, found her gate, and began to look for a restaurant at which we could have breakfast.

Instead of a place more familiar to me, she selected a popular coffee shop. Our morning meal that day did not consist of my customary juice and cereal. Neither did we enjoy coffee, sausage, bacon, pancakes, Danish, or any other favorites. Rather, we dined on currant scones washed down with chai lattés.

Only a few years ago I had never heard of such fare, let alone eaten it. But I have learned to experience and evaluate the new. Many of us have found these to be important skills in a rapidly changing world.

The prophet Jeremiah spoke of God's reliability in such a world. "Because of the Lord's great love we are not consumed, for his compassions never fail. They are new every morning; great is your faithfulness" (Lamentations 3:22, 23).

As we stand at the beginning of another year, we can be assured that we will face new experiences and challenges. Nevertheless, we can also expect them to be balanced with new compassion and new blessings from a never-changing but ever-new God.

Yet those blessings are not ours alone. We have the opportunity to reach others with the hope of a God who anchors us to solid rock while at the same time allows us to explore uncharted waters. With your offerings you are supporting that vision of this congregation.

Make it Your Own

What have you encountered for the first time this year? Substitute that experience for this story to introduce this Scripture.

DATE USED _____

LOVE

In elementary school, we had an annual Valentine's Day card exchange. We would all bring a decorated container to serve as our mailbox. Also, we would bring a card for *every one* of our classmates. No exceptions. No excuses. No one could ever be left out for any reason.

Some cards I loved to give. My best friends would gladly get a card from me. Sure, they were my pals. The cute girls would receive a cardboard proclamation of my attraction to them. Those were easy to write and deliver! But I was obligated by the rules of the class to send greetings to those for whom I had no affection—the class bully, the girl with stringy hair in the second row, the snobbish kid who thought he was better than anyone else—all of them!

As my own private protest, I carefully selected which cards from my assortment I would send to whom. The beautiful cards would go to beautiful people. But how appropriate that the girl I had labeled "horse-face" would get a card with a pony on it! Or that the very large boy with bad breath would receive a cartoon of a gorilla! I met my obligation, but not in the spirit for which the holiday was intended.

To the church in Corinth, Paul addressed the value of giving from wrong motives. "If I give all I possess to the poor and surrender my body to the flames, but have not love, I gain nothing" (1 Corinthians 13:3).

We set aside time each week to give an offering. But what motivates our giving? Are we giving from obligation or out of love?

Make it Your Own

Did you ever give a Valentine's Day gift or a card merely out of obligation? Surely most everyone in the congregation could relate to that story. Try it!

DATE USED _____

UNTHINKABLE

When I was a teenager, my younger sister became predictable in the gifts she would give to me. For my birthday she gave me a flowered, purple shirt. For Christmas, she presented me with a pair of bright purple corduroy slacks. Year after year this pattern continued. Didn't she know that a self-respecting teenage boy wouldn't wear those clothes? But that didn't matter, because *she* would when the gifts were returned to her!

Is this typical of our gift-giving? We may not always give something expecting to get it back, but we still give selfishly. We give as long as it doesn't cost us too much. We give if we have an expectation that the recipient may give even more in return.

What a contrast we find in God's giving. "For God so loved the world that he gave his one and only Son, that whoever believes in him shall not perish but have eternal life" (John 3:16).

The word meaning "one and only" or "only begotten" refers to someone other than Jesus only four times in the New Testament. Isaac (Hebrews 11:17), the widow of Nain's son (Luke 7:12); Jairus's daughter (Luke 8:42); and a certain demon-possessed boy (Luke 9:38) were all "only begottens." It is interesting that in each of these cases, God saw that it was unthinkable for someone to be deprived of a "one and only." In each of these four cases the valuable child was spared. Yet God himself was willing to give more than he would ever expect of others.

On this resurrection Sunday, let us look at our own giving. Do we give out of habit? Do we give because we receive a good feeling for doing so? Do we give expecting recognition from God or from others? Do we give only a fraction of our abundance? Or do we allow God's Spirit to move us to give as he did? Can we be outrageous givers? Can we give to others in ways they could never reciprocate? Can we begin, in some way, to model the unthinkable generosity that is Easter?

Make it Your Own

Consider an example of superficial giving. Has someone given you something "with strings attached?" Have you given a gift that was of far less value than was appropriate? A story like that can be a great contrast to the overwhelming grace of God.

DATE USED _____

94

TAXES

It was my first *real* job. I fried hamburgers at a local fast-food restaurant. And I was about to get my first *real* paycheck.

Anticipating this moment, I had calculated the value of my services countless times. I knew that I had worked 23 hours and that I was to earn a whopping $1.45 per hour. I envisioned the check and its amount, to the very penny.

But when I finally opened my pay envelope, my anticipation turned to confusion. Then confusion turned to rage. Reviewing the itemized deductions that reduced my glorious earnings to a mere shadow of what I had expected, I had only one question. "Who is FICA and why did he take $2.67 of *my* money?!"

Resentment about taxation is nothing new. In fact, Jesus was questioned about that very subject.

"'Tell us then, what is your opinion? Is it right to pay taxes to Caesar or not?'
But Jesus, knowing their evil intent, said, 'You hypocrites, why are you trying to trap

me? Show me the coin used for paying the tax.' They brought him a denarius, and he asked them, 'Whose portrait is this? And whose inscription?'

'Caesar's,' they replied.

Then he said to them, 'Give to Caesar what is Caesar's, and to God what is God's'" (Matthew 22:17-21).

This week in April many people in this country are considering their tax obligation for the year. Each week, however, we have the opportunity of considering the other obligation Jesus mentioned. How much of what we earn should we return to God? May he bless you as you respond to that question at this time.

Make it Your Own

When did you first understand the impact of paying taxes? Begin this meditation with those recollections.

DATE USED _____

VIRTUE

(SUITABLE FOR MOTHER'S DAY)
PROVERBS 31:17-20

For years she has greeted kindergartners as they enter her Sunday school classroom. She patiently listens to their stories, and they listen to hers as she teaches them of the love of the Savior.

She decorates cakes every month and gives them to a local children's home. The sweet tastes in the mouths of the children who celebrate birthdays every month merely shadow the sweetness of her generous and caring heart.

She is a manic gardener who nurtures tomatoes, carrots, peppers, and a host of other vegetables to maturity. Neighbors, friends, relatives, and church members feast upon the results of her labor.

Countless young couples have enjoyed the warmth of her home and the wealth of her dinner table. They have also benefited from the gentle instruction of her example and the guidance of her well-chosen words.

Of all of the gifts she has given I am thankful for one more than any other; she gave me birth.

If I were to characterize my mother by only one of her characteristics, my choice would not be difficult. My mother gives.

In the last chapter of the book of Proverbs the virtuous woman is described. That very characteristic stands out. "She sets about her work vigorously; her arms are strong for her tasks. She sees that her trading is profitable, and her lamp does not go out at night. In her hand she holds the distaff and grasps the spindle with her fingers. She opens her arms to the poor and extends her hands to the needy" (Proverbs 31:17-20).

I am grateful for a mother who has faithfully demonstrated the virtue of generosity. On this day on which we honor our mothers, it is appropriate we consider that example. At this time of stewardship let us demonstrate that we have learned that lesson of selfless giving.

Make it Your Own

Tell about the generosity of your mother. How does she give to others now? How has she been generous to you in the past? Start this meditation with your personal tribute.

DATE USED _____

Remembered

(Suitable for Memorial Day)
Hebrews 6:10

My junior high students had been assigned to write a short essay about a significant figure of the twentieth century. As I looked over the completed assignments, I was generally pleased. Each class member seemed to have an adequate understanding of a particular newsmaker of the past one hundred years.

But my smile of general contentment broke into surprised laughter when I read Justin's conclusions concerning Winston Churchill: "So because of his great leadership, the people of his country considered Winston Churchill to be a great man. When he died they made a statue out of him."

We all would like to be remembered, though maybe not in the way Justin described! This weekend we take time to consider those who have gone before us and have contributed to the blessings we now enjoy.

At times we wonder if we will be remembered. Will the world be a better place because of what we have accomplished here? The writer of Hebrews offers this assurance:

"God is not unjust; he will not forget your work and the love you have shown him as you have helped his people and continue to help them" (Hebrews 6:10).

Our simple acts of caring for others *will* make a difference. Our names may not make the history books, but we have the assurance that God will not forget our acts of love for him shown to his people. As we pause during this time of offering on this Memorial Day weekend, let us consider the legacy that our generosity is creating today.

Make it Your Own

Did you ever have a fractured understanding of a famous person from history? Tell that story here.

DATE USED _____

REWARD

When I think about my dad during my formative years, I remember one characteristic in particular. My father is a man who was always willing to work hard.

His jobs were not easy ones. He labored for years producing aluminum replacement windows. I recall the sharp metal shards that clung to his work clothes. For a time he drove a truck, returning home late each evening, exhausted. At another job he worked in a cabinet-making shop. I remember him reeking of the volatile chemicals used to finish the wood. He breathed those noxious fumes all day long while attempting to earn a living to support a family.

I often wonder how much he wanted to give up. How he must have dreamed of shorter days and longer weekends! Yet his tireless toil provided for a family of which I'm proud to be a part.

In the Old Testament we read of King Asa of Judah. He too, had awesome tasks placed before him. His nation had lapsed into idolatry, and it needed someone to perform the thankless task of turning his people back to

God. A prophet by the name of Azariah encouraged Asa in his task by saying, "But as for you, be strong and do not give up, for your work will be rewarded" (2 Chronicles 15:7).

On this Father's Day it is appropriate to thank our fathers for working so hard on our behalf. Azariah was right. Like King Asa, our fathers' work has had its rewards.

It is also appropriate to look at the results of our work. Our work on behalf of our church will have its rewards in building stronger families, stronger communities, and a stronger nation. We take the opportunity to model the hard work of our fathers as we share in the labor of this church during this time of stewardship.

Make it Your Own

Was your father a hard worker? Honor him with your memories as you introduce these thoughts.

DATE USED _____

FREEDOM

As a principal, I often shared "horror stories" with colleagues at other schools. The time school officials seemed to dread most was the month preceding dismissal for the summer.

My fellow principals related a number of tales that had happened in their schools during that time. Student attention spans shortened dramatically. Grades plummeted. Fights between students became more prevalent. Acts of vandalism increased. Why? Because "freedom" was in sight.

Freedom is a tremendous blessing. Yet that same freedom can be a remarkable curse. The apostle Paul wrote to the Galatians, explaining that in Christ they were free from religious regulation and ritual. What a blessing! Yet he warned them not to allow freedom to be an excuse for uncontrolled behavior. "You, my brothers, were called to be free. But do not use your freedom to indulge the sinful nature; rather, serve one another in love. The entire law is summed up in a single command: 'Love your neighbor as yourself.' If you keep on biting and devouring each other, watch out

or you will be destroyed by each other"
(Galatians 5:13-15).

This week we celebrate our independence as a nation. Our freedom is an enormous blessing. This can be clearly seen in our possessions. Even the poorest among us would be considered unbelievably wealthy in many parts of the world. We are at liberty to use our material goods with little restriction.

But how do we choose to use that freedom? Do we become selfish and attempt to accumulate more for ourselves? Or do we look upon our freedom as a blessing that can be used, in turn, to bless others?

Let us begin our Independence Day celebration right now. Let us commit to using our liberty for the good of others.

Make it Your Own

How have you seen individuals misuse their freedom? It may be an incident you have observed. It may be a story out of the headlines. Either way, share that story to introduce these thoughts.

DATE USED _____

WORK

(SUITABLE FOR LABOR DAY)
EPHESIANS 4:28

What an opportunity! Or so it seemed. . . . In mid-November of my senior year in high school, a neighbor called me with a temporary job offer. For an afternoon's hard labor I would earn three times minimum wage and a steak dinner. I quickly agreed to those terms and reported for work that day.

My task was to help unload a truckload of Christmas trees. I had been warned to dress appropriately, so I donned layers of sweatshirts and heavy work gloves. In spite of my precautions, my four hours of exertion took their toll. In the course of emptying that semitrailer, pine needles savaged my arms, legs, and hands. My limbs were left scratched and bleeding, my muscles exhausted, and my face nearly frostbitten from the gusting north winds in which I toiled. It was probably the hardest physical labor I have ever done. I looked at my paycheck and thought, "Was this worth it? There have to be easier ways of earning a paycheck!"

On this weekend preceding Labor Day, I think back on that Saturday afternoon. I learned what hard work was. But I also learned that there has to be a reason for hard work that transcends merely earning a living. Dollars alone are never enough to make our labor "worth it."

The apostle Paul addressed that issue in his counsel to new believers in Ephesus. As is true today, there were easier ways to gain income than by hard work. Yet there is a higher purpose for such drudgery. Paul commanded, "He who has been stealing must steal no longer, but must work, doing something useful with his own hands, that he may have something to share with those in need" (Ephesians 4:28).

Why do you work? Is it only to have enough for food, clothing, and shelter? If so, you are missing something that will give purpose to the most demanding of tasks. Our God has commanded us to work in order to be a part of something larger. Our work is given a greater significance when we use a portion of it to provide for others.

Make it Your Own

Think about the toughest job you have ever done. Was it worth it? It would make an appropriate introduction to this Labor Day meditation.

Date used _____

FOOD

My mom has always made the best apple dumplings in the world! These glorious confections were filled with sweet, baked apples picked fresh from the trees in our backyard. They were seasoned with cinnamon and wrapped in a golden, flaky crust. Over the entire treat she poured a sticky caramel sauce. My siblings and I would even battle over the gooey remains in the empty pan!

We all have favorite foods. Nothing beats enjoying those foods, with the possible exception of sharing them with people we love. The celebration we look forward to this week is an opportunity to do that.

But it is not a new practice to recognize the goodness of God by eating and sharing food. Centuries ago God saved his nation from a ruthless man of authority in the Persian Empire who wished to exterminate them. In response, the people were called to have an annual celebration commemorating "the time when the Jews got relief from their enemies, and as the month when their sorrow was turned into joy and their mourning into a day of celebration. He

[Mordecai, the cousin of Queen Esther] wrote them to observe the days as days of feasting and joy and giving presents of food to one another and gifts to the poor" (Esther 9:22).

It is interesting to note all of the elements of this celebration. The people feasted. The people gave gifts of food to one another. Those elements are part of our holiday celebrations. But note the third. They also gave gifts to the poor.

How complete are our Thanksgiving plans compared to this standard? Are we merely feasting and sharing with each other, or are we also remembering to give thanks in a very concrete way, by giving to those in need? During this time of stewardship, make your holiday celebration complete. Join with others in this congregation in thanking a saving God by giving to the poor as a part of this offering today.

Make it Your Own

Tell a food story. Tell about your favorite food. Talk about your Thanksgiving Day menu. Then lead into the biblical content.

DATE USED _____

CONTENTMENT

(SUITABLE FOR CHRISTMAS)
1 TIMOTHY 6:6

It was going to be a great Christmas. We had traveled from our home on Christmas Eve to spend the next day with my in-laws. My parents were out of town for the holidays, so we would spend the night at their house, allowing us all of the privacy of a hotel and all of the comforts of home.

I was looking forward to the in-laws doting on my two daughters. I was anticipating talking to relatives I had not seen for more than a year. And, of course, the Yuletide feast was the substance of legends. It was going to be a great Christmas.

Early Christmas morning, however, my prospects began to dim. My seven-year-old woke me with the dreaded pronouncement, "Daddy, I don't feel good. I think I'm sick." Then she promptly presented evidence of her accurate diagnosis on the floor.

Several hours later I sent my wife and younger daughter off to the Christmas feast. I stayed at home with a nauseous, fever-ridden little girl. What a Christmas! No relatives. No celebration. And since my parents were out of town, my mom had taken care not to have groceries spoiling in the refrigerator: no food! By midday I was wallowing in self-pity. Lonely, hungry, and profoundly disappointed, I sat down to my Christmas meal. I was able to find the provisions necessary for a cheese sandwich and tomato soup. Hardly a substitute for what I had expected.

Opening my Bible, I came upon these words from Paul to Timothy, "But godliness with contentment is great gain" (1 Timothy 6:6). "Contentment" is a word we rarely hear during this season. It is a season of long gift lists and high expectations; expectations that are easily dashed, bringing depression and despair.

Make it Your Own

What was your most disappointing Christmas? Did the understanding of a giving God bring you contentment even under those circumstances? That would make a great story to tell.

On that Christmas I considered the mystery of godliness. I recognized that in the midst of a Christmas virtually stripped of all I hoped it would be, the core of the holiday remained. There was profound reason for contentment.

This time of stewardship is an appropriate time to consider what it takes to make us content. Instead of brooding over unmet desires, let us do what God himself did on truly the best Christmas ever. He gave.

DATE USED _____

INDEX OF SCRIPTURES